D0308585

Logical Spelling

B.V. Allan

Illustrated by A. & W. Rodger

Collins : Glasgow and London

Acknowledgements

Childs, S. B. and R. de S. (1966) *Sound Phonics, Sound Spelling, Child's Spelling Rules.* The Educator's Publishing Service Inc., Camb., Mass. Fowler, W. S. (1962) *Fowler's Scientific Spelling.* McDougall's Educational Co., Edinburgh. Lewis, N. (1965) *20 Days to Better Spelling.* Hodder and Stoughton Ltd., London (out of print). Martyn, I. (undated) *Learning to Spell.* Harper, London. Spalding, R. B. (1962) *The Writing Road to Reading.* Whiteside/Morrow, New York.

I am indebted to the above sources and to the ICAA London Word Blind Centre for Dyslexic Children for my initial knowledge of and interest in spelling rules. I am equally indebted to all the children I have taught, in London, Edinburgh, East Lothian and Lancashire, for their co-operation with the wording and arrangement of many of the rules.

First Impression 1977
© 1977 B. V. Allan
0 00 314316 3
Printed in Great Britain

Contents 3

Notes for students

Terms used in this book

apostrophe	As in boy's.
base word	Word without endings. Root word.
capital letter	Large letter, sometimes a different shape from the small letter (e.g. Aa, Bb, Ll). Capital letters are used for *names*. Here are the capital letters : A B C D E F G H I J K L M N O P Q R S T U V W X Y Z
compound word	Two words joined together (e.g. something, classroom).
consonant	Any letter that is not a vowel.
long vowel sound	Any vowel sound that is not a short vowel sound.
medial	In the middle.
plural	More than one (e.g. pigs, dogs).
short vowel sound	hat bed pig dog sun foot **a** **e** **i** **o** **u** **u**
singular	One (e.g. pig, dog).
small letter	Lower case letter. Here are the small letters : a b c d e f g h i j k l m n o p q r s t u v w x y z
syllable	One beat of a word (e.g. ad ven ture has three syllables).
vowel	Sound made with open mouth. There are five vowels : A E I O U. Sometimes we use the letter **Y** instead of **I** as a vowel.

---

1 When small letters are in **bold** type, read their sound, e.g. **f** as in for, **sh** as in ship, **ise** as in sunrise.
2 When a single vowel is a small letter in **bold** type, read its short vowel sound. The short vowel sounds are as in the words :
   hat bed pig dog sun foot
   a   **e**   **i**   **o**   **u**   **u**
3 When capital letters are in **bold** type, e.g. **A B C**, read their name.

Have you learned **1** to **3** above ? These apply in every chapter of **Logical Spelling**.
When you can do **Test A** without any mistakes, you are ready to learn the first rule. Test yourself.

Test yourself Test A

1 A small letter in **bold** type (e.g. **f**) stands for_____
2 A single vowel as a small letter in **bold** type (e.g. **a**) stands for_____
3 A capital letter in **bold** type (e.g. **A**) stands for_____
(Answers on page 6)

Make your own book of rules

You will need   a ring binder, punched loose leaf paper to fit it.

1   First write the chapter title for each chapter in large capital letters in the centre of an empty page.
2   Use a double page for each rule (two pages facing each other). On the left hand page put the number of the rule. Write the rule. Write the words for the rule. Always keep the words in neat columns. *Never copy* the words. You may study each word for as long as you like before writing it from memory.
3   On the right hand page illustrate the rule. Either copy the pictures in the book or make up your own pictures. (Always check first with the teacher that the pictures you want to use *do* illustrate the rule.)
4   When you have finished each chapter, check that your rule numbers are in the right order. See if you can remember the whole chapter of rules off by heart.
5   Keep the rules of every chapter in the same file.

The practice exercises

1   Use an ordinary exercise book for these.
2   Answers are given at the end of each chapter.
3   Answers must always be words that fit the rule.
4   Some exercises must be marked by the teacher.
5   Ask the teacher to check any answers different from those given at the end of the chapter. You may be right!

Writing words

Always
1   Study the word and note any irregularities.
2   Look carefully at the word and say each syllable clearly.
3   Write the word from memory, when you think you know it.
4   Check the word.
5   If it is wrong, relearn it and then rewrite it.
Never
1   Copy the word.
2   Alter the word. (Rewrite any word that is wrong.)
3   Cross out untidily. (A single line through a word tells the reader to ignore that word!)

Words in front of brackets are answers to chapter tests. Words in brackets *and* words in front of brackets are answers to cumulative tests.

Chapter	Rule		Chapter	Rule	

1
1 make face cage
2 blue love (believe)
3 face cage dance
4 little table (semicircle)
5 house (surprise)
6 dance
7 gone

2
1 off ill mess (kisses kill)
2 lick (quick)
3 catch
4 edge
5 stopped
6 middle
7 forgotten
8 travelled
9 borrow
10 sister (little)

3
1 lady slyly baby
2 day boy they boyish
3 babies
4 boyish slyly

4
1 flowers kisses boxes dishes peaches
2 halves
3 tomatoes
4 berries

5
1 quick
2 want squash (quarrel)
3 world

(Chapter 5 continued)
4 cider cycle (semicircle circumference)
5 ginger gym (angel)
6 guest
7 radio
8 find child bolt most

6
1 lady musical cider open nation invasion (babies radio baby believe silent music delicious)
2 house how saw (blow new)
3 murder
4 father
5 ceiling (vein)
6 ask kill
7 table panel quarrel musical (vessel level towel angel label)
8 nation invasion (delicious musician occasion)
9 except (dance)

7
1 anything
2 also until
3 actor
4 musician
5 prize surprise
6 occasion
7 semicircle
8 circumference

Answers to Test A
1 the letter sound
2 the short vowel sound
3 the letter name

Words ending in E

When to put **E** on the end of a word.
Adding endings to words ending in **E**.

Contents

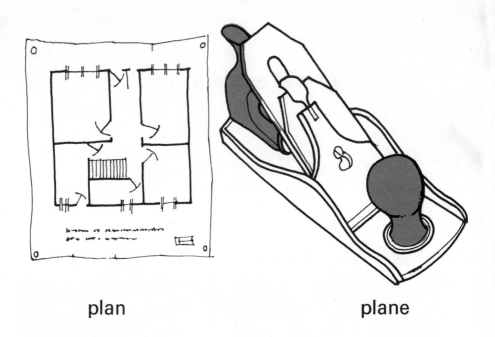

plan   plane

A silent **E** on the end of a word makes the vowel in front say its name.

A-E		I-E		O-E		U-E	
rat	rate	rip	ripe	not	note	cut	cute
hat	hate	Tim	time	hop	hope	hug	huge
fat	fate	rid	ride	pop	Pope	cub	cube
mat	mate	Sid	side	cod	code	tub	tube
man	mane	fin	fine	rod	rode	us	use
pan	pane	pin	pine				
plan	plane	pip	pipe				

Exercise 1

1   Write the rule and words in your file.
2   Learn the rule off by heart. Think about it.
3   Read the words.
4   Say the vowel names.
5   Write down the vowel names in capital letters.

Exercise 2

1 Write these words down the left hand side of the page:

rat	hat	fat	mat	man	pan	plan
rip	Tim	rid	Sid	fin	pin	pip
not	hop	pop	cod	rod		
cut	hug	cub	tub	us		

2 Write the same words with a small e on the end beside them.
3 Read the pairs of words you have made.

Exercise 3

Draw and label these pictures.

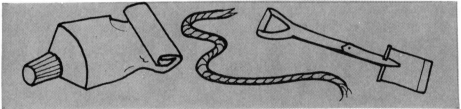

Choose three more words to draw and label.

Exercise 4

Clues   Copy the crossword frame into your book.

Across
1 Past tense of make
3 Bad temper
4 A mole lives in a — — — — in the ground
5 Head of Roman Catholic Church

Down
1 Opposite of female
2 Men made tools of stone in the Stone — — —
3 Used in a tug of war
4 Where we live

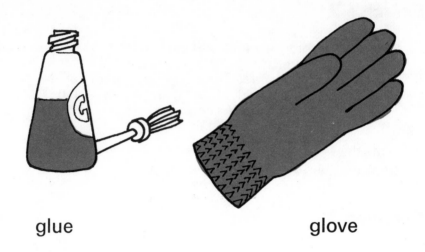

glue   glove

We cannot end a word with **U** or **V**.
We must put **UE** or **VE**.

UE	VE		Note
true	give	curve	the sound **uv**
blue	have	leave	is spelled **OVE**
glue	move	serve	love
sue	live	reserve	dove
issue	sieve	deserve	glove
clue	twelve	forgive	shove
value	deprive	attractive	above

When you are *reading* a word, you do not sound the final **E**. Because there is always an **E** after **U** or **V**, the final **E** gives no clue about the sound of the vowel in front. It may be long or short.

When you are *spelling* a word, *never* end with **U** or **V**. Always put an **E** if the last sound you hear is **u** or **v**.

Exercise 1

1 Write the rule and words in your file.
2 Learn the rule off by heart. Think about it.
3 Read the words.

Exercise 2

Fill in the missing words:
1 I — — — — at home.
2 A gift is something you — — — — to someone.
3 The present tense of had is — — — —.
4 We wear a — — — — — on the hand.
5 A dozen is — — — — — —.
6 When we are sixteen we can — — — — — school.
7 A waiter's job is to — — — — — meals.
8 God will — — — — — — — us our sins.

Exercise 3

Draw and label these pictures.

Choose three more words to draw and label.
Note the sound **uv** is always spelled **OVE**.

Exercise 4

1 Learn this nonsense poem:

Is it true
That glue
Is blue?
Sue will issue
A clue
Of much value
If glue
Is blue.

2 Remember the **UE** on the end of the words.
3 Write down the poem from memory.
4 Check your spellings.

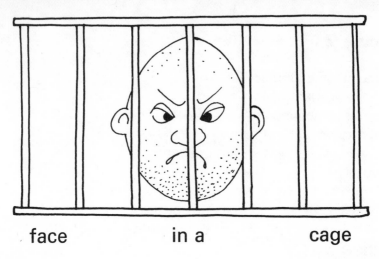

face   in a   cage

E makes C sound s.   **E makes G sound j.**

CE
race
face
place
lace
pace
ice
nice

GE
cage
page
age
rage
wage
huge
large
change

When you are *reading* a word, always read **s** for **CE** and **j** for **GE**.

When you are *spelling* a word, it is hard to know whether to put **CE** or **SE** for the sound **s**. Try to learn the words in the list off by heart.

The **GE** words are easier because we never end a word with the letter **J**. Always put **GE** at the end of a word for the sound **j**.

Exercise 1

1 Write the rule and words in your file.
2 Learn the rule off by heart. Think about it.
3 Read the words.

Exercise 2

The best way to learn a group of words which have the same spelling is to make a poem or sentence, using as few other words as possible.
e.g. The race took place on the face of the nice ice.
Can you fit all the **CE** words into one sentence or poem?

Exercise 3

Draw and label these pictures.

Choose three more words to draw and label.

Exercise 4

Clues   Copy the crossword frame into your book.

Across
2 We tie a shoe with a shoe — — — —
4 A book starts on —— — — —
   one
5 He won the Egg and Spoon
   — — — —
6 Your nose is on your — — — —
7 He was twenty-one years of
   — — —
8 You can skate on it
Down
1 I asked him to keep my
   — — — — — in the queue
3 Same as 7 across
4 A champion runner sets a fast — — — —
5 Another word for bad temper
6 Same as **6** across

candle

The sound **ul** at the end of a word is sometimes spelled **LE**.

little	sparkle
simple	people
apple	dazzle
bubble	battle
treacle	angle
candle	kettle

When you are *reading* a word which ends in **LE**, say **ul**.

When you are *spelling* a word which ends in the sound **ul**, you sometimes put the letters **LE**.

For more **ul** words and spellings, see Chapter 6, Rule 7.

Exercise 1

1 Write the rule and words in your file.
2 Learn the rule off by heart. Think about it.
3 Read the words.

Exercise 2

Fill in the missing words:
1 Water is boiled in a — — — — — —.
2 — — — — — pie is made with apples and pastry.
3 A wax — — — — — — gives us light.
4 When armies meet for one fight it is called a — — — — — —
5 — — — — — — is another word for small.

Exercise 3

Draw and label these pictures.

Choose three more words to draw and label.

Exercise 4

Put the twelve words listed under the rule into alphabetical order.
Can you find any more words?

house   cheese

Singular one-syllable words ending in the sound **s** or **z** end in the letters **SE**.
(This is to distinguish them from plural words which end in **S**.)

s	z
sense	noise
nonsense	poise
horse	pause
else	cause
house	because
mouse	please
purse	these
nurse	those
crease	lose
	choose
	cheese

But	5 words end in **ZE**
	breeze
	freeze
	squeeze
	sneeze
	wheeze

When you are *reading* a word ending in **SE**, say **s** or **z**. Do not pronounce the **E**.

When you are *spelling* a one-syllable word ending in the sound **s** or **z**, put the letters **SE**.

Exercise 1

1   Write the rule and words in your file.
2   Learn the rule off by heart. Think about it.
3   Read the words.

Exercise 2

Five common words break the rule and end in **ZE**:

breeze
freeze
squeeze
sneeze
wheeze

Either   **1** Make up and *learn* a nonsense sentence or poem using these words, remembering all the time that they are **ZE** words.

Or   **2** Learn this nonsense poem: The breeze made him freeze
And sneeze and wheeze
And squeeze his handkerchief.

3 Write down what you have learned. Check your spellings.

Exercise 3

Draw and label these pictures.

Choose three more words to draw and label.

Exercise 4

Put all the twenty words listed under the rule into alphabetical order. (Do not list the exceptions.)

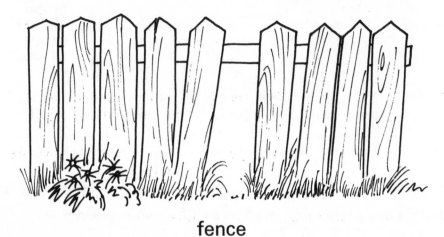

fence

The sound **ns** at the end of a base word is nearly always spelled **NCE**.

dance	bounce		
chance	confidence		
mince	entrance	**But**	sense
dunce	fence		nonsense
once	offence		dense
ounce	defence		

When you are *reading* **NCE** at the end of a word, say **ns**.

When you are *spelling* the sound **ns** at the end of a base word, put **NCE**. (This is to distinguish it from the plural which ends in **S**.)

Exercise 1

1 Write the rule and words in your file.
2 Learn the rule off by heart. Think about it.
3 Read the words.

Exercise 2

Fill in the missing words:
1 To gamble is to take a — — — — — —.
2 We can — — — — — — a rubber ball.
3 A — — — — — is slow at learning.
4 Fairy stories often start with the words "— — — — upon a time."
5 If we say things that do not make sense we are talking
   — — — — — — — —.

Exercise 3

Draw and label these pictures.

Choose three more words to draw and label.

Exercise 4

Clues   Copy the crossword frame into your book.

Across
3 We have — — — — — pies at
   Christmas
4 Ballet is a kind of — — — — —
5 A small weight
Down
1 It is a long time — — — — —
   1066
2 "— — — — upon a time"

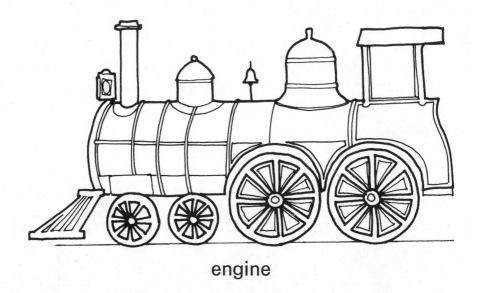

engine

A few words end in 'no job **E**' for no obvious reason. They are usually words which used to be pronounced with the long vowel sound.

come	none	imagine
done	some	genuine
gone	one	promise
		engine

When you are *reading* these words, do not sound the **E**.

Exercise 1

1 Write the rule and words in your file.
2 Learn the rule off by heart. Think about it.
3 Read the words. Learn them off by heart.

Exercise 2

Make up a nonsense story using all the words. Try to use very few extra words.

e.g. *Some* gave a *genuine promise* to *come* when *one engine* had *gone,* but I *imagine* that *none* had *done* this.

The ten 'no job **E**' words have been used with ten other words. Can you make a nonsense sentence using all the 'no job **E**' words and only ten or less extra words?

Exercise 3

Draw and label these pictures.

Choose three more words to draw and label.

Exercise 4

Clues   Copy the crossword frame into your book.

Across
2 Nothing, nil, not any
4 "— — — — here, and I'll give you a sweet"
5 Finished
Down
1 "They have — — — — away"
3 A few
6 Singular

Dropping

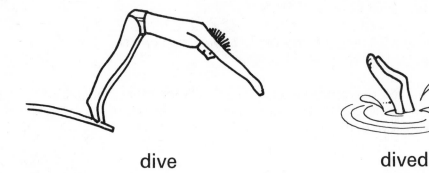

dive   dived

Words ending in a silent **E** drop the **E** before adding an ending beginning with a vowel.

	+**ing**	+**ed**	+**er**	+**en** or **y** or **ous**
hope	hoping	hoped		
ache	aching	ached		
dive	diving	dived	diver	
joke	joking	joked		
live	living	lived		
dare	daring	dared		
serve	serving	served		
paste	pasting	pasted		
rule	ruling	ruled	ruler	
dance	dancing	danced	dancer	
cruise	cruising	cruised	cruiser	
write	writing		writer	
take	taking		taker	taken
make	making		maker	
come	coming			
noise				noisy
fame				famous

Exercise 1

1   Write the rule and words in your file.
2   Learn the rule off by heart. Think about it.
3   Read the words.

Exercise 2

Add the endings **ing** and **er** to these words. Do not copy the words.
First write the list of words to which you are going to add endings.
Head your columns like this:

	+ing	+er
make		
rule		
take		
write		
dance		

Exercise 3

Draw and label these pictures.

Choose three more words to draw and label.

Exercise 4

Fill in the missing words:
1 Tom had — — — — — to win the race.
2 The dancers were — — — — — — — to the music.
3 Most people live in a house, but some people prefer — — — — — —
   in a caravan.
4 The waiter — — — — — — the dinner.
5 He — — — — — into the water head-first.

1

changeable

2

dying   dyeing

We keep final **E** when adding endings

1 To keep the **s** or **j** sound on words ending in **CE** and **GE**.
(Unless the ending begins with **E, I,** or **Y**)

e.g. notice noticed noticing, change changed changing,
race raced racy, mange mangy.

CE		GE	
service	serviceable	change	changeable
peace	peaceable	outrage	outrageous
notice	noticeable	courage	courageous
		advantage	advantageous

2 To clarify meaning.

dye	dyeing
hoe	hoeing
shoe	shoeing

acre	acreage
mile	mileage

Exercise 1

1 Write the rule and words in your file.
2 Learn the rule off by heart. Think about it.
3 Read the words.

Exercise 2

Add these endings.
First write the base word, then alongside it write the word with the
ending added.

service	service	+	**ing**
advantage	advantage	+	**ous**
courage	courage	+	**ous**
race	race	+	**ed**
peace	peace	+	**able**
notice	notice	+	**able**

Exercise 3

Draw and label these pictures.

Choose three more words to draw and label.

Exercise 4

Fill in the missing words:
1   — — — — — — means changing the colour.
2   The blacksmith was — — — — — — — the horse.
3   The gardener was — — — — — — the garden with a big hoe.
4   The — — — — — — — is the number of acres.
5   A car which has only done one thousand miles is said to have a low
    — — — — — — recorded on the clock.

Page

9   **Ex 2**

rat	rate	plan	plane	pin	pine	rod	rode
hat	hate	rip	ripe	pip	pipe	cut	cute
fat	fate	Tim	time	not	note	hug	huge
mat	mate	rid	ride	hop	hope	cub	cube
man	mane	Sid	side	pop	Pope	tub	tube
pan	pane	fin	fine	cod	code	us	use

Ex 3   tube rope spade

Ex 4   *Across* **1** made **3** rage **4** hole **5** Pope *Down* **1** male **2** Age **3** rope **4** home

11   **Ex 2**   **1** live **2** give **3** have **4** glove **5** twelve **6** leave **7** serve **8** forgive

Ex 3   shove love glove

13   **Ex 3**   face cage page

Ex 4   *Across* **2** lace **4** page **5** race **6** face **7** age **8** ice *Down* **1** place **3** age **4** pace **5** rage **6** face

15   **Ex 2**   **1** kettle **2** apple **3** candle **4** battle **5** little

Ex 3   apple kettle people

Ex 4   angle apple battle bubble candle dazzle kettle little people simple sparkle treacle

17   **Ex 3**   horse nurse mouse

Ex 4   because cause cheese choose crease else horse house lose mouse noise nonsense nurse pause please poise purse sense these those

19   **Ex 2**   **1** chance **2** bounce **3** dunce **4** once **5** nonsense

Ex 3   fence entrance dunce

Ex 4   *Across* **3** mince **4** dance **5** ounce *Down* **1** since **2** once

21   **Ex 3**   imagine one engine

Ex 4   *Across* **2** none **4** come **5** done *Down* **1** gone **3** some **6** one

23   **Ex 2**

word	+ing	+er
make	making	maker
rule	ruling	ruler
take	taking	taker
write	writing	writer
dance	dancing	dancer

Ex 3   dancing or dancer ruler cruiser or cruising

Ex 4   **1** hoped **2** dancing **3** living **4** served **5** dived

25   **Ex 2**

service	servicing
advantage	advantageous
courage	courageous
race	raced
peace	peaceable
notice	noticeable

Ex 3   hoeing courageous or outrageous service

Ex 4   **1** dyeing **2** shoeing **3** hoeing **4** acreage **5** mileage

Doubling

Short vowel sounds must be 'shut in'.
Double letters or extra consonants do this.

Note Some letters never double. They are: a h i j
q u v w x y

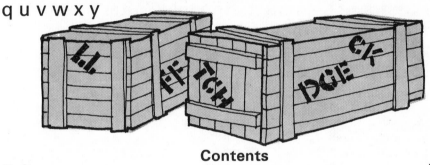

Contents

Rule		Page

cliff   bell   chess

The letters **F**, **L** and **S** are doubled after a single vowel in a one-syllable word.
(The vowel sound is usually short.)

FF	LL		SS	
staff	small	Jill	brass	cross
cliff	tall	gill	class	loss
stiff	bell	hill	grass	moss
whiff	cell	kill	lass	toss
cuff	fell	mill	mass	fuss
huff	hell	quill	pass	
muff	smell	pill	glass	
puff	swell	sill	chess	
stuff	spell	till	cress	
off	tell	still	dress	
	well	doll	less	
	ill	pull	mess	
	bill	full	press	
	fill	dull	bliss	
	shrill	gull	kiss	
	skill	hull	boss	
	drill			

But if
of
has
pal
nil
gas
this
us
yes
thus
bus
plus

And odd
add
egg
inn
ebb
fizz
buzz
jazz

Exercise 1

1 Write the rule and words in your file.
2 Learn the rule off by heart. Think about it.
3 Read the words.

Exercise 2

Fill in the missing words:
1 We ring a — — — —.
2 He paid the — — — —.
3 A person in charge is the — — — —.
4 He fell — — — the — — — — —.
5 Jack and — — — — climbed the — — — —.
6 A window is made of — — — — —.
7 Starch makes things — — — — —.
8 The teacher took all the pupils in her — — — — — to a — — — — —
  band concert.

Exercise 3

Draw and label these pictures.

Choose three more words to draw and label.

Exercise 4

Clues   Copy the crossword frame into your book.

Across
1 Boy's name
3 Small mountains
5 You can ring it
6 Everything
Down
1 Beef comes from a — — — —
2 Not as many
3 Opposite of heaven
4 Not well
5 It is round and it bounces

clock

The sound **k** is spelled **CK** straight after a short vowel sound at the end of a one-syllable word.

back		deck		cock		buck
pack	pack(et)	peck		dock		duck
rack		wreck	wreck(age)	flock		luck
sack		quick		mock		muck
tack		Dick		sock	sock(et)	tuck
whack		lick		pock	pock(et)	truck
shack		flick		rock	rock(et)	struck
track		tick		clock		cuck(oo)
crack		stick		frock		
black						
Jack						

Exercise 1

1 Write the rule and words in your file.
2 Learn the rule off by heart. Think about it.
3 Read the words.

Exercise 2

Read this nonsense poem:
> When the truck
> Struck a duck
> And the cock
> Hit a clock
> I told Dick
> "Just a tick
> Here's a sack
> On the rack
> Put them back
> In the shack."

Write your own nonsense poem, using at least ten words ending in **CK**.

Exercise 3

Draw and label these pictures.

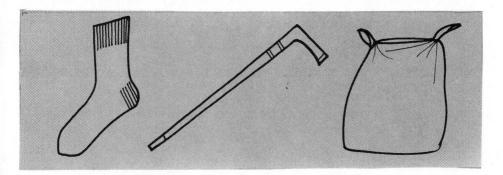

Choose three more words to draw and label.

Exercise 4

Find one or more words for the following: (**CK** words of course!)
1 A colour
2 A boy's name
3 A time piece
4 A bird
5 Dirt
6 Clothing

witch

The sound **ch** is spelled **TCH** straight after a short vowel sound at the end of a one-syllable word.

catch	bitch		
patch	ditch		
match	pitch	**But**	much
watch	witch		such
latch	stitch		duch(ess)
batch	kitch(en)		which
fetch	crutch		rich
wretch			

Note If there is another consonant after the short vowel sound, we only need **CH** e.g. bench lunch larch stench punch parch.

Exercise 1

1   Write the rule and words in your file.
2   Learn the rule off by heart. Think about it.
3   Read the words.

Exercise 2

Put the following in alphabetical order:
catch stitch ditch crutch latch match watch pitch witch patch

Exercise 3

Draw and label these pictures.

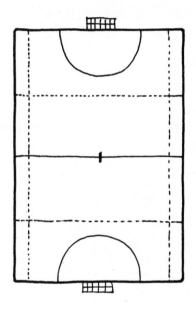 

Choose three more words to draw and label.

Exercise 4

Write one sentence using the common exceptions to this rule.

e.g. Which rich man has much money for such a duchess?

Learn either this sentence or your own, remembering that these words have no **T**.

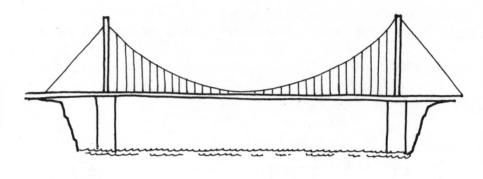

bridge

The sound **j** is spelled **DGE** straight after a short vowel sound at the end of a word.

DGE		
cadge	ridge	judge
badge	bridge	fudge
edge	midge(t)	smudge
ledge	dodge	budge
hedge	lodge	budge(t)
wedge		

Note If there is another consonant after the short vowel sound, we only need **GE**
e.g. hinge plunge
purge singe.

Exercise 1

1 Write the rule and words in your file.
2 Learn the rule off by heart. Think about it.
3 Read the words.

Exercise 2

Fill in the missing words:
1 A — — — — — — goes across a river.
2 We have a privet — — — — — around our garden.
3 A narrow shelf is called a — — — — —
4 He was too weak to — — — — — the heavy stone.
5 Judgement was given by the — — — — —.

Exercise 3

Draw and label these pictures.

Choose three more words to draw and label.

Exercise 4

Clues

Copy the crossword frame into your book.

Across
1 Toboggan
4 Stay in another's house
5 Move slightly
6 Beg
Down
1 Mud
2 Small house at gate
3 Brink
5 Symbol worn on blazer pocket

Doubling consonant

| bat | batter | batting |

In one-syllable words with a short vowel sound we must double the last consonant before adding an ending beginning with a vowel.

PP			
stop	stopping	stopped	stopper
hop	hopping	hopped	hopper
skip	skipping	skipped	skipper
wrap	wrapping	wrapped	wrapper
whip	whipping	whipped	whipper
shop	shopping	shopped	shopper

TT			
hit	hitting		hitter
sit	sitting		sitter
bat	batting	batted	batter
fit	fitting	fitted	fitter
get	getting		
hot	hotter	hottest	
flat	flatter	flattest	

NN			
plan	planning	planned	planner
run	running		runner
fan	fanning	fanned	
pin	pinning	pinned	

GG			
tug	tugging	tugged	
dig	digging		digger
beg	begging	begged	

Exercise 1

1 Write the rule and words in your file.
2 Learn the rule off by heart. Think about it.
3 Read the words.

Exercise 2

Add the endings **ing** and **er** to these words. First write the list
of words and head up your columns, like this:

	+**ing**	+**er**
shop		
hit		
skip		
wrap		
sit		

Add the endings **ing** and **ed** to the following in the same way:

stop   fit   whip   wrap

Add the endings **er** and **est** to the following: flat hot big fit

Exercise 3

Draw and label these pictures.

Choose three more words to draw and label.
Add as many endings as you can to each word (e.g. flat flatter
flattest flatten).

Exercise 4

Put these sentences into the past tense:
1 The fitter fits the wheel.
2 The batter bats well.
3 She stops putting the stopper on.
4 The grasshopper hops away.
5 He wraps the parcel with gilt wrapping.

rabbit

Middle consonants are often doubled after a short vowel sound which is stressed.

dinner	ripple
supper	middle
ribbon	bubble
rabbit	apple
hammer	little
common	penny
cabbage	syllable

But palace

Exercise 1

1 Write the rule and words in your file.
2 Learn the rule off by heart. Think about it.
3 Read the words.

Exercise 2

Put these words in alphabetical order:

middle   penny   hammer   cabbage   dinner   rabbit   common
supper   little   apple

Exercise 3

Draw and label these pictures.

Choose three more words to draw and label.

Exercise 4

Clues   Copy the crossword frame into your book.

Across
3 Small wave
4 Pocket of air (rhymes with
  trouble)
5 A meal
Down
1 A fruit
2 A coin
3 Used to tie hair

begin + **er** = beginner

In words of more than one syllable, if the last syllable has only one vowel, we must double the last consonant before adding an ending beginning with a vowel.
(The vowel sound is usually short.)

permit	permitted	begin	beginning	beginner	
admit	admitted	refer	referring	referred	referral
commit	committed	deter	deterring	deterred	deterrent
omit	omitted	recur	recurring	recurred	
refit	refitted	infer	inferring	inferred	
befit	befitted	incur	incurring	incurred	
forgot	forgotten				
regret	regretted				

Note	We need not double if there are already two consonants
	e.g. disgust disgusting disgusted
	repent repenting repented

Exercise 1

1 Write the rule and words in your file.
2 Learn the rule off by heart. Think about it.
3 Read the words.

Exercise 2

Change these sentences into the past tense:
1 The teacher permits the children to talk.
2 I omit to sign my name.
3 The thief regrets his crime.
4 The beginner refers to his French dictionary.
5 The child admits he is naughty.

Exercise 3

Draw and label these pictures.

Draw and label five more words.

Exercise 4

Read this nonsense rhyme:

A crime I have committed
The beginner admitted
But it is not permitted
My deterrent be omitted
So into jail I'm admitted
For the crime I committed.

Write your own nonsense poem (at least four lines).

quarrel + **ing** = quarrelling

In words of more than one syllable, if the last syllable ends in one vowel plus **L**, we must double the **L** before adding an ending beginning with a vowel.
(The vowel sound is usually short.)

	+ed	+ing	+ic
quarrel	quarrelled	quarrelling	
level	levelled	levelling	
cancel	cancelled	cancelling	
travel	travelled	travelling	
rebel	rebelled	rebelling	
label	labelled	labelling	
tunnel	tunnelled	tunnelling	
shovel	shovelled	shovelling	
signal	signalled	signalling	
metal			metallic

Exercise 1

1 Write the rule and words in your file.
2 Learn the rule off by heart. Think about it.
3 Read the words.

Exercise 2

Add two endings to each of the following words. (First write the word, then write the two words with endings beside it.)

word   **word + ending**   **word + ending**

rebel
level
cancel
quarrel
tunnel
shovel

Exercise 3

Draw and label these pictures.

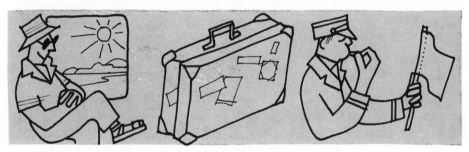

Choose three more words to draw and label.

Exercise 4

Complete these sentences:

1 The match was — — — — — — — — because a team could not be found.
2 — — — — — — — — — — by aeroplane saves time.
3 The enemies often — — — — — — — — — —.
4 The policeman was — — — — — — — — — — for the cars to stop.
5 Their luggage was lost because it was not clearly
   — — — — — — — —.
6 They — — — — — — — — the earth away when they
   — — — — — — — — — underground.

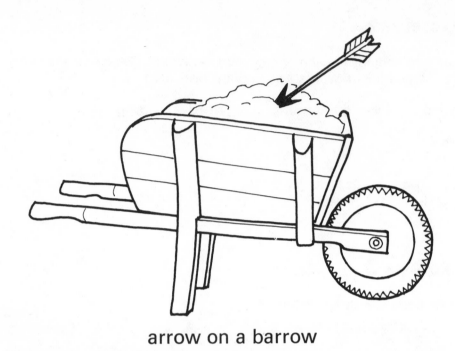

arrow on a barrow

To keep a short vowel sound before **r** we must double the **R**.

barrow	marry	berry	error	horrid
borrow	carry	sorry	terror	horrible
burrow	Harry	lorry	horror	terrible
sorrow	Barry	hurry		arrogant
marrow		curry		arrive
Harrow				
arrow				
tomorrow				

Exercise 1

1 Write the rule and words in your file.
2 Learn the rule off by heart. Think about it.
3 Read the words.

Exercise 2

Read this nonsense poem :
> The terrible boy from Harrow
> Wanted to borrow a barrow
> He made a horrible error
> Causing him terrible terror
> In his great hurry
> And full of curry
> He borrowed a lorry
> Which belonged to Harry
> And was used to carry
> A thousand fleas on a giant marrow.

Write your own nonsense poem, using as many words from the rule as possible.

Exercise 3

Draw and label these pictures.

Choose three more words to draw and label.

Exercise 4

Clues   Copy the crossword frame into your book.

Across
3 Day after today
6 Used with a bow
7 It has one wheel and carries loads
8 To wed
Down
1 Sadness
2 Terrible
4 Vehicle
5 Henry ?

basket

We never double consonants if there are already two

(except before LE e.g. little apple middle saddle).

> sister
> brother
> mother
> winter
> captain
> under
> basket

Exercise 1

1 Write the rule and words in your file.
2 Learn the rule off by heart. Think about it.
3 Read the words.

Exercise 2

Read a page of any book or magazine and note down in separate lists:

1　Words with two different consonants in the middle.
2　Words with double letters followed by **LE**.

Check that all have a short vowel sound before the two different consonants or double letters. (Except vowel sound **a** which may sound **ar** in some dialects.)

Exercise 3

Draw and label these pictures.

Choose three more words to draw and label.

Exercise 4

Put the words found in exercise 2 in alphabetical order.

(If you did not do exercise 2, put the words listed under the rule in alphabetical order.)

Page

29 **Ex 2** **1** bell **2** bill **3** boss **4** off, cliff **5** Jill, hill **6** glass **7** stiff
8 class, brass

Ex 3 cross wall cuff

Ex 4 *Across* **1** Bill **3** hills **5** bell **6** all *Down* **1** bull **2** less **3** hell
4 ill **5** ball

31 **Ex 3** sock stick sack

Ex 4 **1** black **2** Jack, Dick **3** clock **4** cock, duck, cuckoo **5** muck
6 frock, smock

33 **Ex 2** catch crutch ditch latch match patch pitch stitch watch
witch

Ex 3 pitch match watch

35 **Ex 2** **1** bridge **2** hedge **3** ledge **4** budge **5** judge

Ex 3 wedge badge hedge

Ex 4 *Across* **1** sledge **4** lodge **5** budge **6** cadge *Down* **1** sludge
2 lodge **3** edge **5** badge

37 **Ex 2**

shop	shopping	shopper	stop	stopping	stopped
hit	hitting	hitter	fit	fitting	fitted
skip	skipping	skipper	whip	whipping	whipped
wrap	wrapping	wrapper	wrap	wrapping	wrapped
sit	sitting	sitter			
flat	flatter	flattest			
hot	hotter	hottest			
big	bigger	biggest			
fit	fitter	fittest			

Ex 3 shopper whipping batting

Ex 4 **1** The fitter fitted the wheel.
2 The batter batted well.
3 She stopped putting the stopper on.
4 The grasshopper hopped away.
5 He wrapped the parcel with gilt wrapping.

39 **Ex 2** apple cabbage common dinner hammer little middle
penny rabbit supper

Ex 3 bubble dinner hammer

Ex 4 *Across* **3** ripple **4** bubble **5** dinner *Down* **1** apple **2** penny
3 ribbon

41 **Ex 2** **1** The teacher permitted the children to talk.
2 I omitted to sign my name.
3 The thief regretted his crime.
4 The beginner referred to his French dictionary.
5 The child admitted he was naughty.

Ex 3 beginner forgotten

43 **Ex 3** travelling labelled signalled or signalling

Ex 4 **1** cancelled **2** travelling **3** quarrelled **4** signalling **5** labelled
6 shovelled, tunnelled

45 **Ex 3** burrow lorry marrow

Ex 4 *Across* **3** tomorrow **6** arrow **7** barrow **8** marry *Down*
1 sorrow **2** horrid **4** lorry **5** Harry

47 **Ex 3** captain winter basket

Y and I

Y, not **I**, is used at the end of an English word.

Contents

Rule		Page

baby

The sound **i** or **ee** at the end of a word is spelled with the letter **Y**.

lady	boggy	leaky	freely	voluntary
baby	soggy	healthy	creepy	gladly
shaky	frosty	wealthy	beauty	madly
pony	dusty	heavy	majesty	sadly
ivy	fizzy	ready	scarcely	surely
silky	jumpy	spooky	dictionary	lately
rocky	lumpy	thirsty	secretary	immediately
Mary	Harry	Jerry	jolly	bossy
Sally	Barry	Terry	silly	sissy
Betty	Henry	Billy	hilly	sorry

Exercise 1

1   Write the rule and words in your file.
2   Learn the rule off by heart. Think about it.
3   Read the words.

Exercise 2

Read this silly sentence:

Lately a healthy lady gladly held her heavy baby safely on a shaky pony by the ivy.

This sentence has ten words from the rule. Write your own sentence using ten or more words from the rule.

Exercise 3

Draw and label these pictures.

Choose three more words to draw and label.

Exercise 4

Clues

Across
1 Needing a drink
4 To wed
6 Small child
7 A creeper

Down
2 Prepared
3 Boy's name
5 Woman

Copy the crossword frame into your book.

hay   rain   boy   coin

1 The sounds containing final **Y** are used at the *end* of a word.
   OY is also used at the end of a syllable.
2 The sounds with **I** are used in the *middle* of a word.

ay	ai
way	rain
pay	again
say	pain
tray	sail
may	raid
hay	tail
stay	nail
day	chain
today	train
play	

oy	oi
boy	oil
toy	soil
joy	voice
Joy	coin
enjoy	boil
annoy	noise
royal	join
voyage	point
destroy	spoil

Rare	
ey	ei
they	veil
prey	rein
obey	skein
	sleigh
	neigh
	vein
	eight
	their

Exercise 1

1 Write the rule and words in your file.
2 Learn the rule off by heart. Think about it.
3 Read the words.

Exercise 2

Fill in the missing words:
1 'Which — — — do I go ?' asked Her — — — — — Highness.
2 'You must — — — — indoors — — — — —. You cannot
   — — — — — playing in the rain and — — — — — your new coat'
   said — — —.
3 — — — we — — — — all — — —?' asked the two — — —s.

Exercise 3

Draw and label these pictures.

Choose three more words to draw and label.

Exercise 4

Read one page of a book or magazine.
Write down any words ending in the letter **I**.

If you have found any, look them up in the dictionary. You will find
that they are foreign words, probably Italian.
Foreign words should be learned as they are needed.

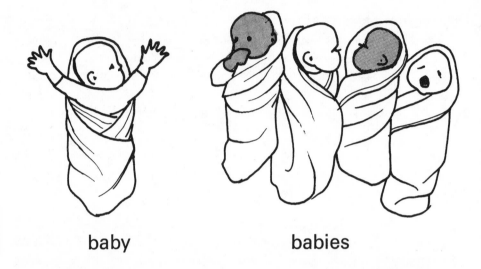

baby   babies

If a word ends in a consonant plus **Y** we change the **Y** to **I** before adding any ending, unless the ending begins with **I**. (We never double **I**).

lady	ladies	hurry	hurries
baby	babies	worry	worries
army	armies	silky	silkiness
party	parties	pretty	prettiness
diary	diaries	heavy	heaviness
library	libraries	carry	carrier
tidy	tidily	worry	worrier
easy	easily	marry	marriage
handy	handily	carry	carriage
		fly	flies
		try	tries
		cry	cries

Exercise 1

1 Write the rule and words in your file.
2 Learn the rule off by heart. Think about it.
3 Read the words.

Exercise 2

Add the ending **ES** to the following:
First list the words, then put the word plus ending alongside it.

> lady
> hurry
> tidy
> worry
> party
> library

Add the ending **AGE** to the following:

> marry
> carry

Exercise 3

Draw and label these pictures.

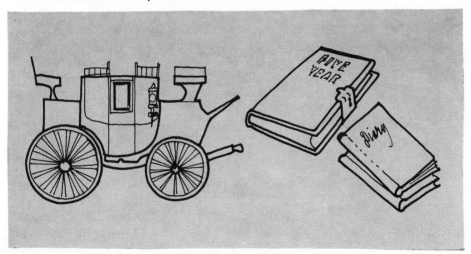

Choose three more words to draw and label.

Exercise 4

Put in alphabetical order the twenty-one words with endings listed under the rule.

paying

shyness

We keep Y before adding an ending:
1   If a word ends in a vowel plus Y.

vowel + Y	ing	ed	er	various
pray	praying	prayed	prayer	
destroy	destroying	destroyed	destroyer	
obey	obeying	obeyed		
prey	preying	preyed		
enjoy	enjoying	enjoyed		
				enjoyable
				enjoyment
boy				boyish
				boyhood
say	saying			
joy				joyous
				joyful

2   If the Y sounds I, before ly and ness.

	ly	ness
dry	dryly	dryness
shy	shyly	shyness
sly	slyly	slyness

But		
	say	said
	pay	paid
	lay	laid
	slay	slain
	day	daily

Exercise 1

1   Write the rule and words in your file.
2   Learn the rule off by heart. Think about it.
3   Read the words.

Exercise 2

Add any one ending to the following words.
First write the words, then put the words plus ending alongside.

dry
say
sly
destroy
pay
shy
boy

Exercise 3

Draw and label these pictures.

Choose three more words to draw and label.

Exercise 4

Clues   Copy the crossword frame into your book.

Across
1 Warship
4 Hunting for food
5 Bashfully
Down
2 Had a good time
3 Following an order

Page

51 **Ex 3** ivy pony lady

   Ex 4 *Across* **1** thirsty **4** marry **6** baby **7** ivy *Down* **2** ready
   3 Terry **5** lady

53 **Ex 2** **1** way, Royal
   2 stay, today, enjoy, spoil, Joy
   3 May, play, day, boys

   Ex 3 toy tray coin

55 **Ex 2** lady   ladies
   hurry   hurries
   tidy   tidies
   worry   worries
   party   parties
   library   libraries
   marry   marriage
   carry   carriage

   Ex 3 carriage diaries

   Ex 4 armies babies carriage carrier cries diaries easily flies
   handily heaviness hurries ladies libraries marriage parties
   prettiness silkiness tidily tries worrier worries

57 **Ex 3** prayer book paying destroyed

   Ex 4 *Across* **1** destroyer **4** preying **5** shyly *Down* **2** enjoyed
   3 obeying

Plurals

Add **S** whenever possible.
Most dictionaries give plurals.

Contents

Rule		Page

buses

After the letters **S**, **X**, **Z**, **SH**, **CH** we add **ES**.

(Adding **ES** always makes an extra syllable so you can *hear* when **ES** is needed.)

bus	buses	six	sixes	catch	catches
pass	passes	box	boxes	match	matches
stress	stresses	fox	foxes	watch	watches
kiss	kisses	buzz	buzzes	peach	peaches
miss	misses	lash	lashes	stitch	stitches
boss	bosses	wash	washes	ditch	ditches
loss	losses	dish	dishes	coach	coaches
toss	tosses	fish	fishes	roach	roaches
		wish	wishes	church	churches
		cosh	coshes		
		dash	dashes		

Exercise 1

1 Write the rule and words in your file.
2 Learn the rule off by heart. Think about it.
3 Read the words.

Exercise 2

Make these words plural.
First write the word, then put its plural alongside it.

word	plural
bus	
fox	
kiss	
chest	
buzz	
match	
mat	
fish	
church	
rag	

Exercise 3

Draw and label these pictures.

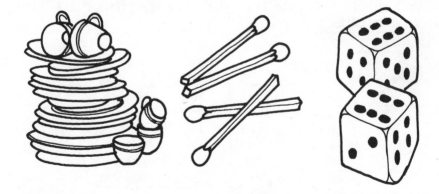

Choose three more words to draw and label.

Exercise 4

Can you remember which letters need **ES** for the plural?
Write them down across the top of the page.
Write as many words under each column as you can remember without
looking at the list under the rule.

leaf   leaves

When a word ends in **F** we change the **F** to **VE** before adding plural **S**.

loaf	loaves
leaf	leaves
calf	calves
half	halves
wolf	wolves
life	lives
thief	thieves

elf	elves
self	selves
shelf	shelves
wife	wives
knife	knives
scarf	scarves

Exercise 1

1 Write the rule and words in your file.
2 Learn the rule off by heart. Think about it.
3 Read the words.

Exercise 2

Change all singular words into plural :
1 The life of a wolf is like that of a thief.
2 The calf ate a loaf off the shelf.
3 The boy enjoyed himself in the garden.
4 His wife wears a scarf round her neck.

Exercise 3

Draw and label these pictures.

Choose three more words to draw and label.

Exercise 4

Read this silly rhyme :
    We like
    Halves
    Of calves,
    Said the elves
    To themselves.
    But we like knives,
    Said the wives
    To themselves.
Write your own silly rhyme using as many words from the rule as
possible.
Learn either this rhyme or your own.
Write it down from memory.

tomato   tomatoes

Some words ending in a consonant plus **O** add **ES** to form the plural.

tomato	tomatoes	mosquito	mosquitoes
potato	potatoes	torpedo	torpedoes
volcano	volcanoes	veto	vetoes
echo	echoes	embargo	embargoes
hero	heroes	innuendo	innuendoes
Negro	Negroes		

But Some just add **S**

pianos
solos
manifestos

Exercise 1

1 Write the rule and words in your file.
2 Learn the rule off by heart. Think about it.
3 Read the words.

Exercise 2

Complete these sentences :
1 Performances by one person are called — — — — —.
2 — — — — — — — — — — are insects that bite.
3 — — — — — — — — — — sometimes erupt.
4 The music shop sold many grand — — — — — —.
5 We eat — — — — — — — and — — — — — — — — —.

Exercise 3

Draw and label these pictures.

Choose three more words to draw and label.

Exercise 4

Read one page of a book or magazine.

Head your page with two columns, **OS** and **OES**.

List any relevant words from the page you read under the correct column.

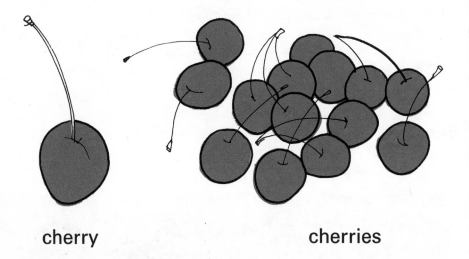

cherry   cherries

If a word ends with a consonant plus **Y** we change the **Y** to **I** and add **ES** for the plural.

lorry	lorries	cherry	cherries	spy	spies
lady	ladies	berry	berries	fly	flies
baby	babies	ferry	ferries	cry	cries
penny	pennies	bunny	bunnies	ally	allies
bully	bullies	party	parties	try	tries
				rely	relies
				reply	replies
				supply	supplies

Exercise 1

1 Write the rule and words in your file.
2 Learn the rule off by heart. Think about it.
3 Read the words.

Exercise 2

Make these words plural.
First write the word, then put the plural alongside it.

word	plural
fly	
bunny	
cry	
berry	
sky	
ferry	
cherry	

Exercise 3

Draw and label these pictures.

Choose three more words to draw and label.

Exercise 4

Clues

Copy the crossword frame into your book.

Across
1 Enemy agents seeking our secrets
5 Friendly nations
6 They grow on holly
Down
2 Coins
3 Noises of distress
4 Insects

Numbers, letters, signs

3's   X's   +'s

To make numbers, letters and signs plural we add apostrophe **S**.

1's	A's	+'s
2's	B's	−'s
3's	C's	×'s
etc.	etc.	÷'s
		%'s

Exercise 1

1 Write the rule and words in your file.
2 Learn the rule off by heart. Think about it.
3 Read the words.

Chapter 4   Answers

Page
61   **Ex 2**

bus	buses	match	matches
fox	foxes	mat	mats
kiss	kisses	fish	fishes
chest	chests	church	churches
buzz	buzzes	rag	rags

   Ex 3 dishes, matches, sixes
   Ex 4 See word list under rule.
63   **Ex 2** 1 The lives of wolves are like those of thieves.
               2 The calves ate loaves off the shelves.
               3 The boys enjoyed themselves in the gardens.
               4 Their wives wear scarves round their necks.
   Ex 3 loaves leaves halves
65   **Ex 2** 1 solos 2 Mosquitoes 3 Volcanoes 4 pianos 5 tomatoes, potatoes
   Ex 3 pianos tomatoes volcanoes
67   **Ex 2**

fly	flies	sky	skies
bunny	bunnies	ferry	ferries
cry	cries	cherry	cherries
berry	berries		

   Ex 3 lorries, pennies, cherries
   Ex 4 *Across* 1 spies 5 allies 6 berries *Down* 2 pennies 3 cries 4 flies

Sounds altered by certain letters

Contents

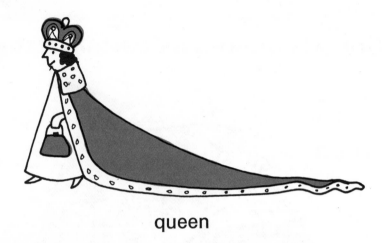

queen

The letter **Q** has no sound by itself. We always put
QU and it sounds **kw**.
QU must be followed by a vowel.

quick	quake	query	equerry
quiz	quite	quell	request
queen	queasy	quill	inquest
queer	quote	quiver	require
quench	quotation	quirk	enquire
quibble	quiet	qualm	bequeath
quarrel	quest	quizzical	
quaint	question	querulous	
		quail	

Note not **kw**
queue
quay

Exercise 1

1 Write the rule and words in your file.
2 Learn the rule off by heart. Think about it.
3 Read the words.

Exercise 2

Read this silly sentence:

The queer, quaint queen quivered and quaked quietly when questioned about her quarrel with a queasy quail.

It uses ten **QU** words.
Write your own silly sentence using ten or more **QU** words.

Exercise 3

Draw and label these pictures.

Choose three more words to draw and label.

Exercise 4

Put these words in alphabetical order:

quill quail quote queen quaint quiet quake quite

squashed wasp

The sound **o** after **W** is spelled with the letter **A**.

was	wallop	warrant	warranty
want	wasp	wad	
wash	wallet	wan	
watch	waddle	swan	
wand	waffle	swamp	
wander		swallow	

Note w(h)at

The sound **o** after **QU** (sounds **kw**) is spelled with the letter **A**.

quad	quantity	squat
quash	quality	squash
quarry	qualify	squad
quarrel	quarantine	squalid
squadron	squabble	squander

Exercise 1

1 Write the rule and words in your file.
2 Learn the rule off by heart. Think about it.
3 Read the words.

Exercise 2

Find at least two words for each of the following :
1   Birds
2   Verbs
3   Arguments
4   Groups of men in the army

Exercise 3

Draw and label these pictures.

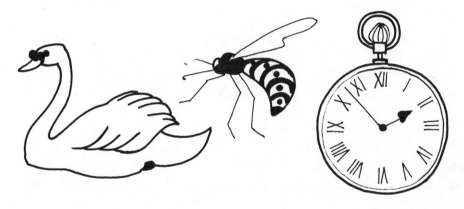

Choose three more words to draw and label.

Exercise 4

Clues   Copy the crossword frame into your book.

Across
3 Past tense of is
5 Isolation of infectious people
6 Insect with a sting
Down
1 A bird
2 Argue
3 Desires
4 Crush
6 Lump of material

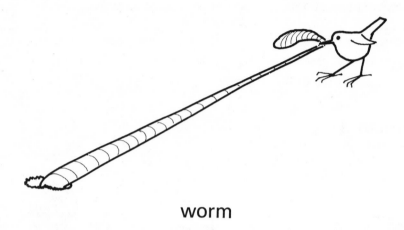

worm

The sound **wer** is spelled **WOR**.

worm	worth	worthy		
word	worship	wort		
world	worse	worst		
wormwood	work	worker	working	worked

But

were

Exercise 1

1 Write the rule and words in your file.
2 Learn the rule off by heart. Think about it.
3 Read the words.

Exercise 2

Read this silly sentence:

The world's worst worm worthily working worships with wormwood and wort.

All the words from the rule are used. Write your own silly sentence. Try to use all the words.

Exercise 3

Draw and label these pictures.

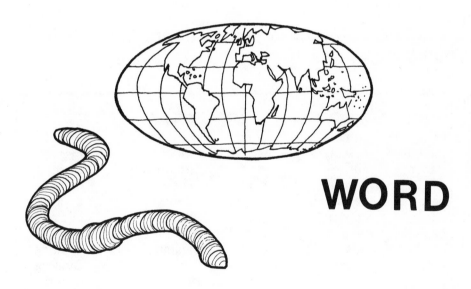

WORD

Choose three more words to draw and label.

Exercise 4

Put all the words listed under the rule in alphabetical order.

(Including all variations of the same base word—e.g. work, worker, working, worked—but not the exception. There are fourteen words.)

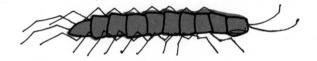

centipede

If single **C** is followed by the letters **E, I** or **Y** it sounds **s**.

CE		CI		CY
cell	cellar	circus	cinema	cycle
cent	cement	circle	cinnamon	bicycle
recent	cemetery	recite	cipher	cygnet
decent	censor	cider	circumstance	cymbal
century	census	cigar	cistern	cynic
cease	centipede	cinder	citadel	cypress
cedar	centre	excited	city	cyclamen
ceiling	certain	pencil	civil	cyclist
celebrate	peace	icing	civilian	cyclone
celery	except			Cyclops
nice	grocer			cylinder
mice	ice			fancy
once	slice			Lucy
piece				

Exercise 1

1 Write the rule and words in your file.
2 Learn the rule off by heart. Think about it.
3 Read the words.

Exercise 2

Complete these sentences:
1 A — — — — — — is a room below a house.
2 A — — — — — — — has two wheels.
3 We call a hundred years a — — — — — — —.
4 We go to a — — — — — — to see films.
5 A large town with a cathedral is called a — — — —.
6 A young swan is called a — — — — — —.
7 — — — — — is an alcoholic drink made from apples.
8 A portion of cake may be called a — — — — —.

Exercise 3

Draw and label these pictures.

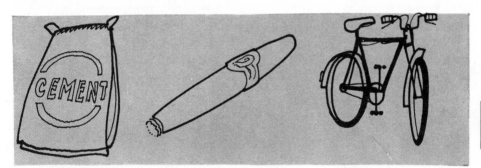

Choose three more words to draw and label.

Exercise 4

Clues   Copy the crossword frame into your book.

Across
2 Pleasant
5 A plant
7 London is one
Down
1 Two wheeled vehicle
3 To stop
4 Used for garage floor
6 Polite

cage   giraffe   gymnastics

If single **G** is followed by the letters **E, I** or **Y** it *often* sounds **j**.

GE		GI	GY	Note	
cage	generation	gin	gym	tiger	giggle
page	genuine	ginger	gymnastics	geese	gild
huge	genius	giraffe	gymnasium	gear	gill
large	genial	giant	gypsy	gelding	gilt
Geneva	geometry	gist	gyrate	get	gimlet
George	geography	gigantic	Egypt	geyser	gift
gem	geology	Reginald		girl	gingham
general	germ			gibbon	girder
generous	Germany			giddy	girdle
gentle	gesture			give	begin
				gig	

Exercise 1

1 Write the rule and words in your file.
2 Learn the rule off by heart. Think about it.
3 Read the words.

Exercice 2

Find at least two words for each of the following :
1 Animals
2 Subjects learned at school
3 Countries
4 Boys' names

Exercice 3

Draw and label these pictures.

Choose three more words to draw and label.

Exercice 4

Put the exceptions to this rule in alphabetical order.

Remember that these twenty-one common words *break* the rule. You will already know most of them.

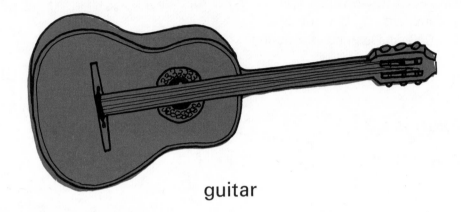

guitar

To spell the sound **g** before the letters **E**, **I** or **Y** we often put **GU**.

guess	guide	guinea
guest	guild	Guinness
guelder	guilt	guitar
guerilla	guile	guilty
Guernsey	guise	beguile
guy	guillemot	disguise
Guy	guillotine	

But 1 All the exceptions to Rule 5 on page 78.

2 guard
guarantee

Exercise 1

1 Write the rule and words in your file.
2 Learn the rule off by heart. Think about it.
3 Read the words.

Exercise 2

Complete these sentences:

1 A — — — — — — — — — is a sea bird.
2 People — — — — — — of murder used to be hanged.
3 A — — — — — — — — — — — is used for beheading.
4 He wore a mask to — — — — — — — — himself.
5 A — — — — — — was worth one pound, one shilling.
6 — — — — — — — — — is a name for stout.
7 The — — — — — showed us the way.
8 There were ten — — — — —s at the party.

Exercise 3

Draw and label these pictures.

Choose three more words to draw and label.

Exercise 4

Clues Copy the crossword frame into your book.

Across
1 Musical instrument
2 One who stays at another's house
5 Hide one's identity
Down
1 A Channel Island
2 Person who shows one the way
3 Try to answer without knowing
4 Put on top of a bonfire

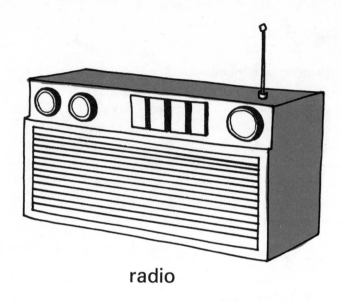

radio

To spell the sound **i** or **ee** before a vowel we use the letter **I**.

radio	radius
radiator	obvious
Indian	experience
radiant	material
Ian	

Note also

IGUE	IQUE	INE
intrigue	antique	machine
fatigue		submarine
		gelatine
		margarine

Exercise 1

1 Write the rule and words in your file.
2 Learn the rule off by heart. Think about it.
3 Read the words.

Exercise 2

Put all the words listed under the rule in alphabetical order. (Including **Note also** there are sixteen words.)

Exercise 3

Draw and label these pictures.

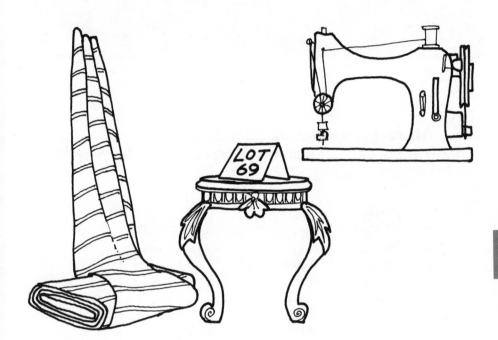

Choose three more words to draw and label.

Exercise 4

Read one page of a book or magazine.

List all the words containing the letter **I** sounding **i** or **ee** followed by a vowel.

Note The **I** must have the sound **i** or **ee**. e.g. in the word 'action', the letter **I** does not fit this rule.

ghost

The letters **l** and **O** *sometimes* sound their names before **ND**, **LD**, **LT**, or **ST** in one-syllable words.

ND	LD	LT	ST
bind	child	bolt	most
blind	mild	jolt	ghost
find	wild		post
grind	old		host
kind	hold		
mind	bold		
rind	cold		
wind	fold		
behind	gold		
remind	scold		
	told		
	sold		
	mo(u)ld		

Exercise 1

1 Write the rule and words in your file.
2 Learn the rule off by heart. Think about it.
3 Read the words.

Exercise 2

The word 'blind' has two meanings.
Write two sentences for each of the following words to illustrate two different meanings. You may use your dictionary.

kind	gold
mind	mould
mild	post
hold	bolt

Exercise 3

Draw and label these pictures.

Choose three more words to draw and label.

Exercise 4

Clues   Copy the crossword frame into your book.

Across
2 Brave
4 In the rear
6 Send a letter
Down
1 Not young
2 Join together
3 Spirit
4 Eat food fast
5 Nearly all

Page
71   **Ex 3**   quill queue quarrel
        Ex 4   quail quaint quake queen quiet quill quite quote
73   **Ex 2**   **1** swan, swallow
        2 was, want, wash, watch, wander, wallop, waddle, waffle, swamp, swallow, warrant, squash, quarrel, qualify, squabble, squat, quash, squander
        3 quarrel, squabble
        4 squad, squadron
        Ex 3   swan wasp watch
        Ex 4   *Across* **3** was **5** quarantine **6** wasp *Down* **1** swan **2** quarrel **3** wants **4** squash **6** wad
75   **Ex 3**   worm world word
        Ex 4   word work worked worker working world worm wormwood worse worship worst wort worth worthy
77   **Ex 2**   **1** cellar **2** bicycle **3** century **4** cinema **5** city **6** cygnet **7** Cider **8** piece, slice
        Ex 3   cement cigar bicycle
        Ex 4   *Across* **2** nice **5** cyclamen **7** city *Down* **1** bicycle **3** cease **4** cement **6** civil
79   **Ex 2**   **1** giraffe, tiger, gelding, gibbon
        2 geometry, geography, geology, German, gymnastics
        3 Germany, Egypt
        4 George, Reginald
        Ex 3   giant gem gypsy
        Ex 4   begin gear geese gelding get geyser gibbon giddy gift gig giggle gild gill gilt gimlet gingham girder girdle girl give tiger
81   **Ex 2**   **1** guillemot **2** guilty **3** guillotine **4** disguise **5** guinea **6** Guinness **7** guide **8** guests
        Ex 3   guitar guy guide
        Ex 4   *Across* **1** guitar **2** guest **5** disguise *Down* **1** Guernsey **2** guide **3** guess **4** guy
83   **Ex 2**   antique experience fatigue gelatine Ian Indian intrigue machine margarine material obvious radiant radiator radio radius submarine
        Ex 3   material antique machine
85   **Ex 3**   post gold bolt
        Ex 4   *Across* **2** bold **4** behind **6** post *Down* **1** old **2** bind **3** ghost **4** bolt **5** most

Which spelling?

Clues as to which spelling to use when we have a choice of different spellings for the same sound.

Contents

ba con   re ward   spi der   ho tel   tu lip

To spell the sounds **A**, **E**, **I**, **O** and **U** at the end of a syllable we usually just put the letters **A**, **E**, **I**, **O** and **U**.

A	E	I	O	U
baby	even	silent	open	music
navy	remain	spider	over	tulip
lady	repeat	china	hotel	pupil
gravy	report	pirate	moment	student
bacon	because	giant	total	stupid
apron	beside	Friday	October	uniform
April	believe	lilac	November	tunic
radio	decide	quiet		usual
radiator	deliver	cider		usually
lazy	reward			Lucy
Amy	December			lupin
				January
				February
				July

Exercise 1

1   Write the rule and words in your file.
2   Learn the rule off by heart. Think about it.
3   Read the words.

Exercise 2

Write at least two words for each of the following:
1 Children at school
2 Months
3 People
4 Clothing
5 Not noisy

Exercise 3

Draw and label these pictures.

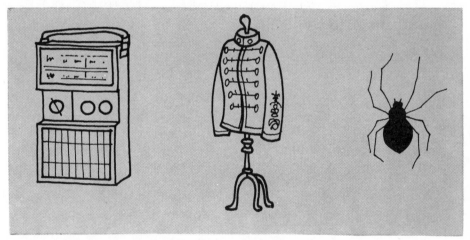

Choose three more words to draw and label.

Exercise 4

Clues

Copy the crossword frame into your book.

Across
2 Sum
4 Idle
5 Summer flower
Down
1 As expected
2 Spring flower
3 Girl's name

cow   house

1 The sounds containing final **W** are used at the end of a word or syllable, and before final **N**.

2 The sounds containing final **U** are used in the middle of a syllable.

ow	ou
cow	house
how	mouse
now	found
bow	ground
powder	round
flower	sound
owl	about
clown	out
town	count
brown	mountain

aw	au
saw	haul
raw	launch
straw	autumn
awful	August
draw	laundry
law	cause
lawyer	sauce
sawn	saucer
lawn	caution
prawn	
drawn	
yawn	

ow		oa
low	narrow	boat
blow	yellow	coat
show	crow	coal
know	snow	throat
slow	blown	load
bow	shown	soap
fellow	known	roast
follow	flown	toast
arrow		coach

ew	oo
flew	room
chew	soon
drew	zoom
new	fool
stew	moon
knew	roof
grew	hoof
threw	food
blew	boot
yew	school
hew	
hewn	

Exercise 1

1 Write the rule and words in your file.
2 Learn the rule off by heart. Think about it.
3 Read the words.

Exercise 2

Write the eight sounds across your page.
Read a page of a book or magazine and enter in the correct columns
all words containing these sounds.
If any words break the rule, note them down.

Exercise 3

Draw and label these pictures.

Choose three more words to draw and label.

Exercise 4

Fill in the missing words:
1 We get milk from a — — —.
2 He — — — — out the candle.
3 A rose is a — — — — — —.
4 The archer — — — — — away his — — — and — — — — —.
5 Autumn leaves are — — — — — and — — — — — —.

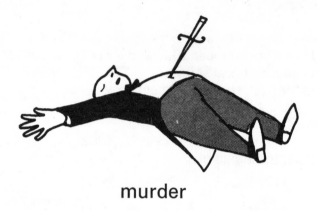

murder

The sound **er** is often spelled **UR** when stressed.
(At the end of a word **ER** is most common.)

UR		ER
further	turkey	after
murder	Thursday	bother
curtain	purpose	sister
turnip	return	brother
burglar	hurtle	supper
turbine	turtle	dinner
purple	turgid	hammer
		dimmer

Exercise 1

1 Write the rule and words in your file.
2 Learn the rule off by heart. Think about it.
3 Read the words.

Exercise 2

Read this silly sentence :

On Thursday, the purposeful purple burglar murdered a turtle and a turkey and hurtled the curtain over the turbine and returned further on to eat his turnip.

Write your own silly sentence, using the **UR** words listed on page 92.

Read it aloud to a friend and check that each **UR** syllable is the one that is stressed.

Exercise 3

Draw and label these pictures.

Choose three more words to draw and label.

Exercise 4

Put the fourteen **UR** words listed under the rule in alphabetical order.

basket

The sound **ar** is spelled with the letter **A** if it is followed by two consonants.

(**Note** This rule is not needed in areas where this sound is pronounced **a**, except in the words 'rather' and 'father'.)

father	ask
rather	basket
mast	mask
past	task
last	gasp
fast	clasp
after	pass
craft	grass
	grasp

Note	Some words have a silent **L** instead of **AR**
	calm
	calf
	palm
	half
	psalm
	qualm

Exercise 1

1 Write the rule and words in your file.
2 Learn the rule off by heart. Think about it.
3 Read the words.

Exercise 2

This nonsense sentence uses all the **AL** (sounded **ar**) words :

Half a calm calf sat in a palm singing a psalm without a qualm.

Write your own nonsense sentence, using all the **AL** words. Learn either this sentence, or your own.

Write it from memory. (Remember all the words have the **AL** spelling.)

Exercise 3

Draw and label these pictures.

Choose three more words to draw and label.

Exercise 4

Clues

Copy the crossword frame into your book.

Across
1 Later in time
4 Succeed in an exam
5 Daddy
Down
2 Work to be done
3 Slightly

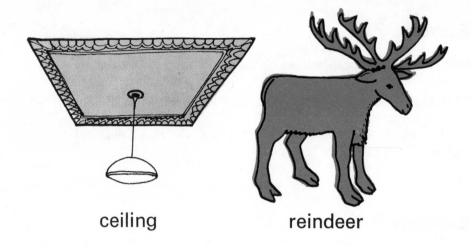

ceiling   reindeer

We use the letters EI
1 For the sound **ee** after the letter **C**.

CEI	
ceiling	conceit
deceive	deceit
receive	perceive
receipt	

2 Sometimes for the sound **A**.

EI = A	
vein	rein
veil	reign
deign	weigh
feign	neigh
sheik	reindeer
surveillance	weight
eight	neighbour
freight	
sleigh	

But	neither
	seize
	forfeit
	leisure
	their
	counterfeit
	foreign
	sovereign

Exercise 1

1 Write the rule and words in your file.
2 Learn the rule off by heart. Think about it.
3 Read the words.

Exercise 2

Fill in the missing words:

1 Blood is carried through the — — — —s.
2 We say a vain person is — — — — — — —ed.
3 My next door — — — — — — — — —   — — — — —s ten stones.
4 Two fours are — — — — —.
5 — — — — — — — pull Santa's — — — — — —.
6 A — — — — — — — — —   — — — — —s over his people.

Exercise 3

Draw and label these pictures.

Choose three more words to draw and label.

Exercise 4

Put all the twenty-three words listed under the rule in alphabetical order, leaving out the exceptions.

cat   kettle

We put **C** for the sound **k** whenever possible.

e.g. cap cat catch cot copy collar scratch scrape scream act sect duct cup cupboard cube cuckoo.

We need K
1   Before **E**, **I** and **Y** to keep the **k** sound.
2   After another consonant at the end of a word.

1 E, I and Y			2 at end	But
kettle	make	kite	ask	kangaroo
kennel	shake	kitten	task	skate
Kent	take	kiwi	mask	kale
kerb	lake	kimono	walk	kaleidoscope
keep	mistake	kin	talk	kali
key	kill	kind	stalk	kaolin
kernel	kipper	kindle	chalk	koala
kestrel	kick	king	thank	Koran
ketch	kid	kink	rank	kosher
ketchup	kidnap	kiosk	bank	skua
kelp	kidney	kiss	ink	skull
keg	kiln	skin	sink	skulk
kemp	kilt	kylin	think	skunk
Kenneth	kit	kymograph	ark	
handkerchief	kitchen	kyanize	bark	
			shark	

Exercise 1

1 Write the rule and words in your file.
2 Learn the rule off by heart. Think about it.
3 Read the words.

Exercise 2

Write at least two words for each of the following:
1 Food
2 Articles of clothing
3 Baby animals
4 Birds

Exercise 3

Draw and label these pictures.

Choose three more words to draw and label.

Exercise 4

Clues   Copy the crossword frame into your book.

Across
1 Move on ice
4 Dog's home
6 It covers the body
Down
2 Boy's name
3 Japanese robe
4 English county
5 Areas of water

table   barrel   comical

The sound **ul** at the end of a base word is often spelled **LE**.

e.g. table bubble candle riddle rifle angle sparkle pickle apple title little dazzle gentle

1 After the letters **N**, **R**, **S**, **V**, **W**, soft **C** and soft **G** we put **EL**.

after **N**	after **R**	after **S**	after **V**	after **W**	after **G** (**j**) and **C** (**s**)	others
panel	quarrel	vessel	level	towel	angel	label
channel	barrel	tassel	travel	vowel	cancel	chapel
tunnel		diesel	shovel	trowel		model
funnel				jewel		pastel
kennel						duel

2 Where it means 'to do with' the word in front we put **AL**.

musical	topical	universal
accidental	mechanical	biblical
personal	normal	physical
comical	coastal	mental
seasonal	theatrical	

Exercise 1

1 Write the rule and words in your file.
2 Learn the rule off by heart. Think about it.
3 Read the words.

Exercise 2

Put the twenty-four words listed under section **1** of the rule in alphabetical order.

Exercise 3

Draw and label these pictures.

Choose three more words to draw and label.

Exercise 4

Fill in the missing words:
1 The comic is — — — — — — —.
2 Things of the universe are — — — — — — — — — —.
3 — — — — — — — areas are by the coast.
4 Things belonging to a person are — — — — — — — —.
5 Things happening by accident are — — — — — — — — — —.

invention   explosion   magician

To spell the sound **sh** at the beginning of all syllables except the first we put **TI**, **SI** or **CI**, (*not* **SH**).

TI	SI	CI
nation	invasion	social
ambition	occasion	ancient
invention	explosion	conscience
information	session	electrician
composition	admission	magician
examination	procession	delicious
ambitious	permission	suspicious
preferential		gracious
fictitious		
cautious		
infectious		

But	fashion
	cushion

Exercise 1

1 Write the rule and words in your file.
2 Learn the rule off by heart. Think about it.
3 Read the words.

Exercise 2

Head three columns **TI SI CI** across the top of your page.

Read a page of a book or magazine. Write all the **TI**, **SI** and **CI** words under the correct column.

Exercise 3

Draw and label these pictures.

Choose three more words to draw and label.

Exercise 4

Fill in the missing words:

1 Churchill was — — — — — — — — — — that a German
  — — — — — — — — — of our — — — — — — was imminent.
2 The — — — — — — — — — — — asked — — — — — — — — —
  to turn off the electricity.
3 Measles is an — — — — — — — — — disease.
4 The — — — — — — — — — of the atomic bomb resulted in a
  massive — — — — — — — — —.

exceed

pence

We spell the sound **s**
1 **C** after **X**

except
excite
excitement
excellent
exceed
excess
excel
excise
excerpt

Note The sound **z** after **X** requires no **C**

e.g. exist
example
exercise

2 **CE** after **N**

once	lance
since	prance
mince	enhance
prince	dance
wince	fence
dunce	pence
ounce	sentence
bounce	pretence
entrance	excellence
chance	

But sense
nonsense
dense
immense

Exercise 1

1 Write the rule and words in your file.
2 Learn the rule off by heart. Think about it.
3 Read the words.

Exercise 2

This silly sentence uses eleven of the **NCE** words:

The dunce bounced as he danced at the entrance fence and winced at paying six pence for an ounce of mince since once it was three pence an ounce.

Write your own silly sentence using at least ten **NCE** words.

Exercise 3

Draw and label these pictures.

Choose three more words to draw and label.

Exercise 4

Clues   Copy the crossword frame into your book.

Across
1 Railing
3 Be more than
4 Do better than
5 An extract
Down
2 Rouse
3 Duty charged

Chapter 6
Answers

106

Page

89 Ex 2   **1** pupil, student
       2 April, December, October, November, January, February, July
       3 baby, lady, Amy, pirate, giant, pupil, student, Lucy
       4 apron, uniform, tunic
       5 silent, quiet

    Ex 3   radio uniform spider

    Ex 4   *Across* **2** total **4** lazy **5** lupin *Down* **1** usual **2** tulip **3** Amy

91 Ex 3   clown stew straw

    Ex 4   **1** cow **2** blew **3** flower **4** threw, bow, arrow **5** brown, yellow

93 Ex 3   turkey hammer curtain

    Ex 4   burglar, curtain, further, hurtle, murder, purple, purpose, return, Thursday, turbine, turgid, turkey, turnip, turtle

95 Ex 3   mask grass craft

    Ex 4   *Across* **1** after **4** pass **5** father *Down* **2** task **3** rather

97 Ex 2   **1** veins **2** conceited **3** neighbour, weighs **4** eight **5** reindeer, sleigh **6** sovereign, reigns

    Ex 3   receipt sleigh reindeer

    Ex 4   ceiling, conceit, deceit, deceive, deign, eight, feign, freight, neigh, neighbour, perceive, receipt, receive, reign, rein, reindeer, sheik, sleigh, surveillance, veil, vein, weigh, weight

99 Ex 2   **1** kernel, ketchup, kipper, kidney
       2 cap, collar, handkerchief, kilt, kimono, mask
       3 kid, kitten
       4 kestrel, kite, kiwi, skua

    Ex 3   kipper kennel kiosk

    Ex 4   *Across* **1** skate **4** kennel **6** skin *Down* **2** Kenneth **3** kimono **4** Kent **5** lakes

101 Ex 2   angel barrel cancel channel chapel diesel duel funnel jewel kennel label level model panel pastel quarrel shovel tassel towel travel trowel tunnel vessel vowel

    Ex 3   apple towel label

    Ex 4   **1** comical **2** universal **3** coastal **4** personal **5** accidental

103 Ex 3   station procession magician

    Ex 4   **1** suspicious, invasion, nation
       2 electrician, permission
       3 infectious
       4 invention, explosion

105 Ex 3   dunce pence fence

    Ex 4   *Across* **1** fence **3** exceed **4** excel **5** excerpt *Down* **2** excite **3** excise

Prefixes and suffixes

Contents

class + room = classroom

Compound words retain the full spelling of both words.

someone	withheld
anyone	uphill
anything	toward
something	backward
knowledge	classroom
upset	timetable

Exercise 1

1 Write the rule and words in your file.
2 Learn the rule off by heart. Think about it.
3 Read the words.

Exercise 2

Read a page of a book or magazine. Write down any compound words you find.
Check that they all retain the full spelling of each word.

Exercise 3

Draw and label these pictures.

Choose three more words to draw and label.

Exercise 4

Fill in the missing words:

1   'Has — — — — — — seen — — — — — — — — — about the bus times in the — — — — — — — — — ?' asked the traveller.
2   He climbed — — — — — —   — — — — — — the top of the hill.
3   Teachers try to impart — — — — — — — — — in the — — — — — — — — — .
4   The spy was — — — — — when the enemy agent — — — — — — — — — valuable — — — — — — — — — about — — — — — — — — — of vital importance.

alone

The words ALL, WELL, FULL and TILL always drop
one **L** when added to another word.

always	welcome	awful	until
already	welfare	wonderful	
almost		helpful	
also		useful	
alone		cheerful	
although		beautiful	

Exercise 1

1 Write the rule and words in your file.
2 Learn the rule off by heart. Think about it.
3 Read the words.

Exercise 2

Put the fifteen words listed under the rule in alphabetical order.

Exercise 3

Draw and label these pictures.

Choose three more words to draw and label.

Exercise 4

Clues

Copy the crossword frame into your book.

Across
3 Nearly
4 Though
6 Up to, before
7 By oneself

Down
1 As well
2 Health, well being
5 Same as 6 across

actor

We use the ending **OR** when the word means 'one who' or 'that which'.

actor	error	**But**	soft **C** and **G** take **ER** to keep the **s** and **j** sound	a simple verb ending in **E** becomes **ER**
director	governor			
ambassador	inspector			
ancestor	instructor			baker
author	inventor			
bachelor	professor		grocer	maker
collector	successor		avenger	writer
competitor	survivor			
conqueror	traitor			

Exercise 1

1 Write the rule and words in your file.
2 Learn the rule off by heart. Think about it.
3 Read the words.

Exercise 2

Fill in the missing words:

1 One who acts is an — — — — —.
2 One who inspects is an — — — — — — — — —.
3 One who bakes is a — — — — —.
4 One who governs is a — — — — — — — — —.
5 One who avenges is an — — — — — — —.
6 That which is wrong is an — — — — —.
7 One who betrays his country is a — — — — — — — —.
8 One who writes books is an — — — — — —.

Exercise 3

Draw and label these pictures.

Choose three more words to draw and label.

Exercise 4

Put the eighteen **OR** words listed under the rule in alphabetical order.

magician

If an ending means 'to do with' or 'a person who', the neutral vowel is usually **A**.

al	ant	ar
comical	attendant	angular
musical	assailant	calendar
global	sergeant	circular
spherical	lieutenant	consular
seasonal		muscular
		scholar
		liar

ary	ance	an
dictionary	attendance	musician
centenary	inheritance	electrician
literary	insurance	magician
parliamentary	vengeance	
library	acquaintance	
	remittance	

Exercise 1

1 Write the rule and words in your file.
2 Learn the rule off by heart. Think about it.
3 Read the words.

Exercise 2

Read a page of a book or magazine. List any words that fit this rule.

Arrange them in columns like the words listed under the rule.

Exercise 3

Draw and label these pictures.

Choose three more words to draw and label.

Exercise 4

Find at least two words for each of the following:
1   Round
2   Army people
3   To do with words
4   Performers

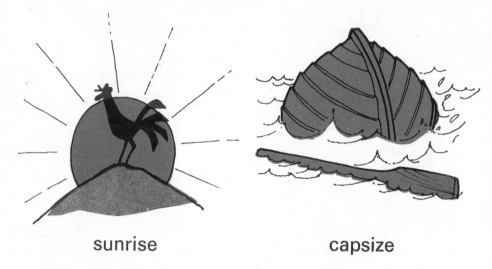

sunrise   capsize

The sound **ize** at the end of a word can almost always be spelled **ISE**.

ISE	
advertise	realise
sunrise	tantalise
despise	appetise
supervise	dramatise
advise	baptise
exercise	organise
surmise	authorise
chastise	apologise
surprise	recognise
utilise	economise
sympathise	

But	IZE	YSE
	prize	analyse
	capsize	paralyse
	assize	
	tranquillize	
	hypnotize	
	mesmerize	

Exercise 1

1   Write the rule and words in your file.
2   Learn the rule off by heart. Think about it.
3   Read the words.

Exercise 2

Put all the words listed under the rule in alphabetical order. (Including the exceptions, there are twenty-nine words.)

Exercise 3

Draw and label these pictures.

Choose three more words to draw and label.

Exercise 4

Find at least two words for each of the following :
1   Put into an artificial sleep, under another's power
2   Be sorry
3   Nouns
4   Do on television

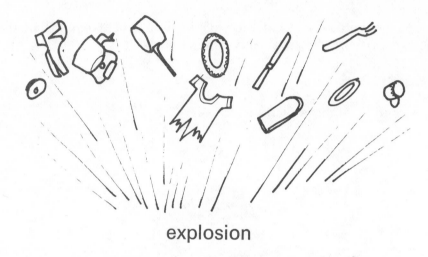

explosion

The sound **zhon** at the end of a word is spelled **SION**.

occasion	abrasion
cohesion	collusion
dissuasion	inclusion
intrusion	delusion
persuasion	fusion
explosion	confusion
invasion	profusion
revision	decision
vision	adhesion
division	circumcision
provision	seclusion
television	derision
incision	illusion

Exercise 1

1 Write the rule and words in your file.
2 Learn the rule off by heart. Think about it.
3 Read the words.

Exercise 2

Put the twenty-six words listed under the rule in alphabetical order.

Exercise 3

Draw and label these pictures.

Choose three more words to draw and label.

Exercise 4

Clues

Copy the crossword frame into your book.

Across
1 Reconsideration
4 A sharing
6 A false impression
7 T.V. stands for
  tele— — — — —
8 A blending

Down
2 Encroachment
3 A sticking together
5 A birthday is a special
  — — — — — — —

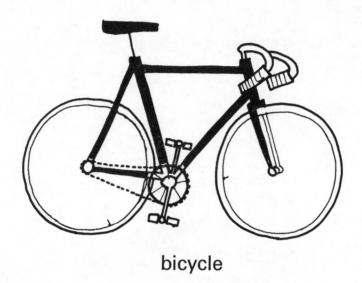

bicycle

Prefixes ending with a vowel do not change their spelling before a base word.

a	(on, to, towards, into, in, away, up, out, from, without)
ante	(before)
anti	(against)
bi	(two, twice)
de	(from, down, away, completely, un-)
di	(twice, double, through, across)
re	(again, back)
pre	(before)
pro	(forth, in place of, for, before)
peri	(around)
se	(apart, without)
semi	(half)
tri	(three)

Exercise 1

1 Write the rule and words in your file.
2 Learn the rule off by heart. Think about it.
3 Read the words.

Exercise 2

Choose five prefixes listed under the rule. Use your dictionary to find four words containing each.

Make sure that the prefix *is* the beginning of the word. (Words beginning with the same letters may not be using the prefix. You will need to look at the meaning and also at the base word.)

Exercise 3

Draw and label these pictures.

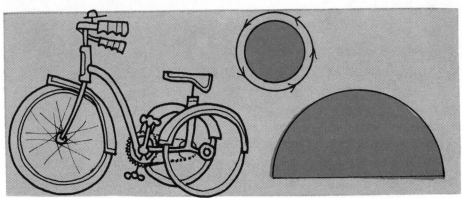

Choose three more words to draw and label.
(Possibly from exercise 2)

Exercise 4

Fill in the missing prefixes:
1　A — —cycle is a two-wheeled vehicle.
2　A — — — —scope is used in a submarine for seeing above the water.
3　A room leading into another room is called an — — — —room.
4　To — —turn is to go back.
5　A — — —pod is a stand on three legs.
6　An — — — —dote is a medicine which counteracts poison.
7　To — — —claim is to announce publicly.
8　To — —base is to lower the quality.

underwater

The following prefixes which end with a consonant do not change their spelling before a base word.

(**Note** some are also words so apply also to Rule 1, Compound words.)

circum	(around)
inter	(between)
mis	(wrongly, badly)
out	
over	
post	(after)
sub	(under)
super	(over, beyond)
trans	(across, beyond)
un	(negative, contrary)
under	

Exercise 1

1 Write the rule and words in your file.
2 Learn the rule off by heart. Think about it.
3 Read the words.

Exercise 2

Write a sentence using each of the following words:

1	circumference	6	international
2	overtake	7	transatlantic
3	underneath	8	supernatural
4	mistake	9	posthumous
5	unnecessary	10	outrageous

Exercise 3

Draw and label these pictures.

Choose three more words to draw and label.
(Use your dictionary).

Exercise 4

Fill in the missing prefixes:
The — — — — —national — — — — —atlantic flight — — — — — —
navigated the airport with its — — — — —carriage ready for landing.
The pilot — — —calculated, however, and — — — —shot the runway.
He heard through the — — — — —com that — —less he could gain
height quickly, he would regret his — — —take and the — — —come of
his — — —judgement could be disastrous.

Page

109   **Ex 3**   uphill classroom timetable
      Ex 4   **1** anyone, anything, timetable
              2 uphill, toward
              3 knowledge, classroom
              4 upset, withheld, knowledge, something

111   **Ex 2**   almost alone already also although always awful beautiful cheerful helpful until useful welcome welfare wonderful
      Ex 3   welcome beautiful alone
      Ex 4   *Across* **3** almost **4** although **6** until **7** alone *Down* **1** also **2** welfare **5** until

113   **Ex 2**   **1** actor **2** inspector **3** baker **4** governor **5** avenger **6** error **7** traitor **8** writer, author
      Ex 3   baker grocer professor
      Ex 4   actor ambassador ancestor author bachelor collector competitor conqueror director error governor inspector instructor inventor professor successor survivor traitor

115   **Ex 3**   musician circular sergeant
      Ex 4   **1** global, spherical, circular
              2 sergeant, lieutenant
              3 dictionary, literary, library
              4 musician, magician

117   **Ex 2**   advertise advise analyse apologise appetise assize authorise baptise capsize chastise despise dramatise economise exercise hypnotize mesmerize organise paralyse prize realise recognise sunrise supervise surmise surprise sympathise tantalise tranquillize utilise
      Ex 3   prize baptise exercise
      Ex 4   **1** hypnotize, mesmerize
              2 sympathise, apologise
              3 sunrise, exercise, surmise, surprise, prize, assize
              4 advertise, dramatise

119   **Ex 2**   abrasion adhesion circumcision cohesion collusion confusion decision delusion derision dissuasion division explosion fusion illusion incision inclusion intrusion invasion occasion persuasion profusion provision revision seclusion television vision
      Ex 3   division television explosion
      Ex 4   *Across* **1** revision **4** division **6** delusion **7** vision **8** fusion *Down* **2** invasion **3** adhesion **5** occasion

121   **Ex 3**   tricycle perimeter semicircle
      Ex 4   **1** bicycle **2** periscope **3** anteroom **4** return **5** tripod **6** antidote **7** proclaim **8** debase

123   **Ex 3**   undertaker postscript superstition
      Ex 4   international, transatlantic, circumnavigated, undercarriage, miscalculated, overshot, intercom, unless, mistake, outcome, misjudgement

1 Place the words under the relevant rule.
If a word fits two or more rules, put it under each one.

Chapter 1   house   gone   make   little   face   dance
cage   table   blue   love

Chapter 2   catch   edge   off   stopped   ill   forgotten
mess   sister   borrow   travelled   lick   middle

Chapter 3   lady   babies   slyly   day   baby   boyish   boy   they

Chapter 4   kisses   berries   flowers   halves   boxes
tomatoes   peaches   dishes

Chapter 5   bolt   cider   quick   cycle   most   squash
world   child   guest   ginger   radio   gym
find   want

Chapter 6   lady   except   table   nation   ask   invasion
kill   panel   cider   house   ceiling   how
father   saw   quarrel   open   musical   murder

Chapter 7   occasion   circumference   anything   surprise
actor   prize   semicircle   also   musician
until

Cumulative   anything   make   babies   silent   blue
boyish   open   love   slyly   music   face
flowers   how   also   cage   kisses   saw
little   boxes   blow   murder   new   dishes
house   dance   peaches   father   gone
halves   ceiling   off   prize   tomatoes   vein
ill   surprise   kill   ask   berries   table
semicircle   until   mess   quick   panel   lick
want   quarrel   catch   circumference
squash   want   vessel   level   edge   towel
stopped   angel   cider   label   middle
cycle   actor   musical   forgotten   ginger
nation   travelled   gym   musician   invasion
guest   except   delicious   borrow   radio
sister   find   lady   day   child   occasion
bolt   most   baby   they   believe   until

2 A teacher or a friend can dictate the words as a spelling test.

(Answers on page 6)

Notes for teachers

1 The rules need not be presented in the order in which they appear in the book. With small groups a rule should be taught as the need for it arises, thus establishing an immediate connecting link and illustrating the value of the rule and how it can simplify the spelling of similar words. With large classes, however, it may be necessary to teach the rules systematically, working through the chapters.
The rules are grouped in chapters to enable the pupil to see logical connections between them. Each pupil should start by writing the chapter headings as described in the **Notes for students** (page 4). Ensure that a whole page is used for each title and that the writing is large and clear. As each rule is taught it is numbered and placed in the correct chapter in the file. Finding this is part of the exercise in seeing logical connections between rules, so do not tell the pupil where to put it.

2 **Logical Spelling** is not designed for any one particular age group. I have taught these rules to children of seven to adults of twenty-seven (for both reading and spelling purposes). The practice exercises are deliberately simple. This is not an insult to older students and adults. The sole purpose of them is to practise the words and the rules. The simpler the exercise, the greater the concentration on the words and rules.
Illustrations are deliberately simple outline drawings to encourage the student to visualise for himself. Exercises asking the student to illustrate a word are for the same reason. This process is as valuable to older students as to younger ones. Many poor spellers lack visualising skills.

3 Teach the **Notes for students** section thoroughly, and ensure that rules are being read correctly and properly understood. Establish good habits of word memorisation from the start. *Never* allow word copying, alterations or sloppy handwriting in the spelling lesson.
Intelligent pupils may well work through the book on their own. Such pupils do not need the book ! It is up to you, the teacher, to explain the rules and encourage good work habits among the majority of your students.

4 As each rule is taught, test each student individually for understanding of the rule.
Each rule should then be learned off by heart. Present the rule and words to the group and let them write them on to file paper (ensuring that each word is written from memory). Check each rule as it is completed and encourage the student to check it. Only after checking should the student be allowed to learn the rule off by heart. When he can say it to you without prompting, can read the word lists correctly and has shown that he understands it, he is ready to do the practice exercises.

5 Keep a record of the rules taught. If a student subsequently mis-spells a word for which he has learned the relevant rule, refer him to his file. Do not tell him which rule covers the word. At first he may need to read through all the rules he has done. Later he will use the chapter headings as clues. Eventually he may recall the rule and correct the word without reference to the file.

6 It is important to ensure that a word is never copied. The pupil should always be allowed to study a word as long as necessary saying each syllable clearly, then write it from memory. He should then check the word. If it is wrong he should restudy it and try again. This process should be repeated as often as necessary.

7 To aid future recall of a word, the word should always be written in joined handwriting. Encourage the pupil to write a whole word at a time.

8 The whole course of **Logical Spelling** could be used over several years. It is devised for use both in the primary and the secondary school. Continuity of use is vital so it is important that teachers at each stage consult one another in its use.
The pupils should be encouraged to keep their 'Spelling File' through-out the school, and their record of work done should be carried forward from year to year.

9 These rules were collected as the need for them arose to explain the reading and spelling of the words involved, and to simplify many words often thought to lack any system. They were collected in chapter form to ease retention by using logical connections within rules. Approximately eighty per cent of English words are regular according to some pattern.

10 Word lists and exceptions are not exhaustive. Extra words fitting each rule should be entered as they arise.

11 Spelling rules *can* be made fun and if you explain to the students that learning rules is easier and quicker than learning each word separately they do not find them such a burden.

12 Merely knowing the rule is only the first step to spelling mastery. It is the constant referral to a rule learned that brings mastery. The pupil has to learn the rule first but it is only when writing a word reminds him of the relevant rule that the rule can help him.

13 Typing the rules and words is helpful to many students. An appeal to parents or local firms often brings a free typewriter.

14 All exercises involving sentences should be answered by writing the full sentence. Crossword frames should be copied or traced into the student's exercise book.

15 Answers are given at the end of each chapter. A different answer is allowable provided it fits the rule. Where answers are not given, the exercise can only be corrected by a teacher.

16 A few rules are affected by dialect.
 a Chapter 2 Rule 7 can be simplified in areas where the vowel before **R** is pronounced as a short vowel sound.
 b Chapter 6 Rule 3 can be omitted in areas where the **U** is pronounced **u**.
 c Chapter 6 Rule 4 can be omitted in areas where the words given are pronounced with short vowel sounds. (But the **AL** words could be taught.)